THE
SEVEN
WONDERS
OF THE NATURAL WORLD

Reg Cox & Neil Morris

Illustrated by James Field & Simone End

Chelsea House Publishers
Philadelphia

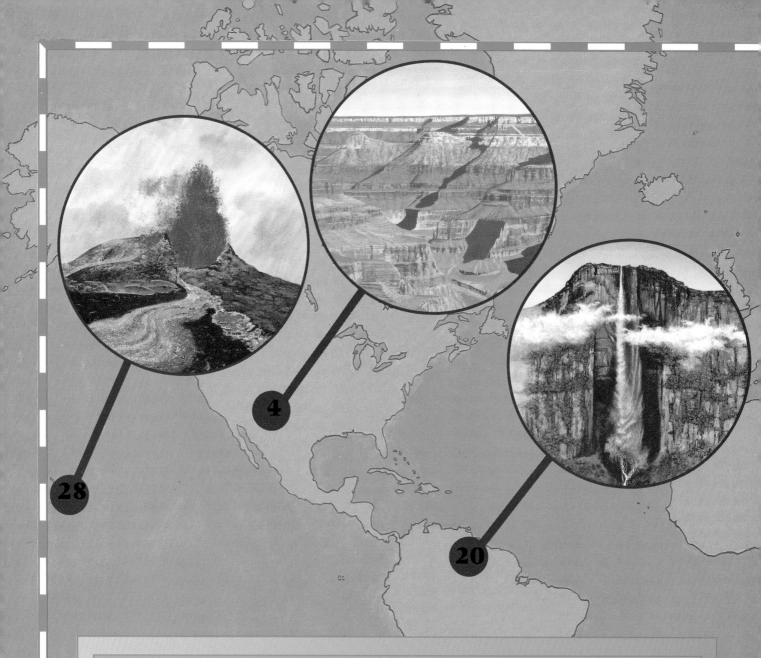

28

4

20

Introduction

Over 2,000 years ago, a Greek poet wrote about some of the most amazing buildings and statues of his time. His list of the Seven Wonders of the Ancient World has survived to this day. But no such list exists for the world's greatest natural wonders. Planet Earth is so amazing and so varied that it is not easy to limit its treasures to seven examples. Those chosen for this book are really nature's extremes. They are earth's largest desert, gorge, reef, cave, and volcano, plus the highest mountain and waterfall. These natural wonders are not only vast and beautiful, they also tell us much about the history of our planet. Although each wonder has existed for a long time, none has been frozen in time. Each one has changed over thousands and millions of years. Human beings are relative newcomers to the planet and still have a lot of fascinating things to learn about earth's greatest wonders.

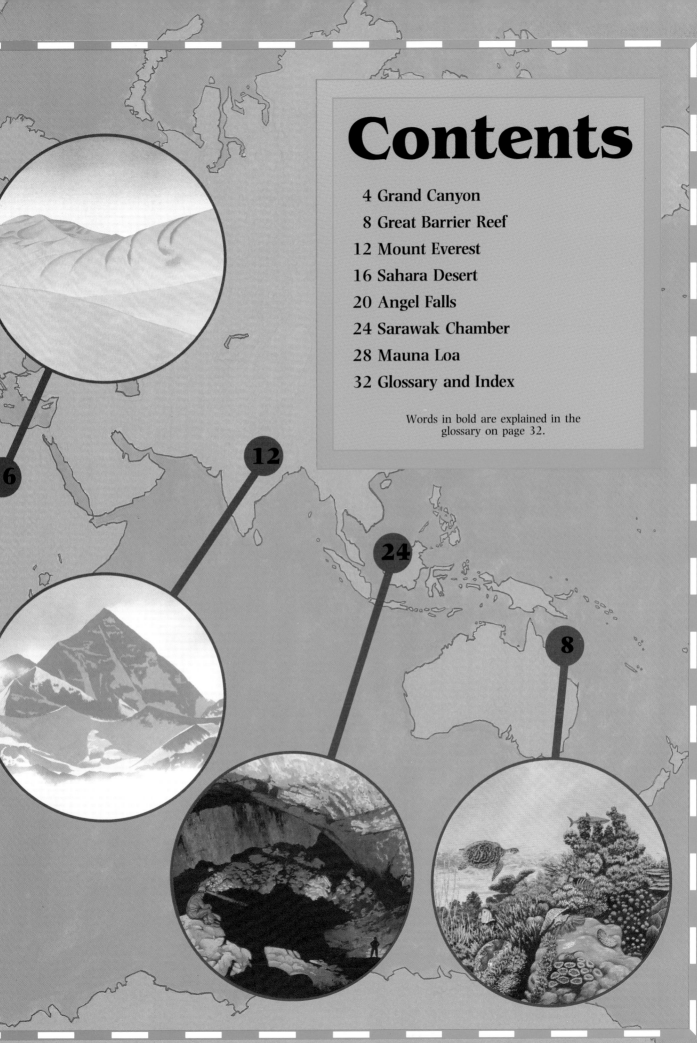

Contents

Words in bold are explained in the glossary on page 32.

16

12

24

8

Grand Canyon

This vast gorge, in Arizona, U.S., is easily the largest in the world. In places the Grand Canyon plunges to a depth of 5,250 feet, and at its widest point it is 18 miles across. The Colorado River flows through the gorge's entire length, on its way from the Rockies to the Gulf of California.

WORLD HERITAGE

The Grand Canyon is one of the world's most spectacular natural features. It is also important to scientists studying the history of the world. In 1919 the Grand Canyon became a United States **National Park**, and in 1979 it became a World **Heritage** Site, because of its scientific importance.

HISTORY THROUGH ROCKS

The walls of the Grand Canyon let us look back over millions of years. The rocks at the bottom of the Canyon are 2,000 million years old. At that time they formed the floor of an ancient ocean. Over hundreds of millions of years, layers of different-colored sandstone, **shale**, and limestone rocks were deposited on top.

Around 60 million years ago—just after the age of the dinosaurs—two rivers flowed through the rock bed, wearing away the rocks and forming a gorge. When the rivers came together to form the Colorado, the rushing water had even more power to loosen sandy gravel and carve out a deeper gorge.

DEEPENING THE GORGE

As the river carved a route through the rocks, movements in the earth's **crust** made the gorge even deeper. Extreme summer heat, winter winds, frost, and rain helped to make the cracks wider. No wonder people once believed that the canyon had been cut open by a giant earthquake. The many layers of rock range in color from pale yellow to dark red. This gives the Grand Canyon a wondrous appearance that changes with the light.

A CHANGE IN THE WEATHER

The canyon is so deep that there are different types of weather within it. The highest parts of the gorge are covered in snow throughout the winter. The North Rim is the coldest area, with snowfalls of up to 10 feet in an average winter. Yet on the floor of the canyon, the river flows through a hot desert landscape.

LIFE IN THE CANYON

Though the canyon looks barren, the changing climate allows many different kinds of plants and animals to survive. There are over 1,000 different flowering plants and at least 300 species of birds. Near the top of the gorge, there are spruce and aspen trees. At the bottom, where it is much hotter, the most common plants are cacti. Gray foxes and chipmunks live on the cooler walls of the gorge, while skunks, lizards, and scorpions prefer the desert **scrub** on the canyon floor.

NATIVE AMERICAN SETTLERS

The first people to see the Grand Canyon were Native Americans who arrived in the area around 11,000 years ago. Today a small area of the Grand Canyon has been set aside as a **reservation** for the few remaining Havasupai Indians. These herders and farmers have lived along the Colorado River for hundreds of years.

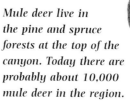

Grand Canyon

The Colorado River winds its way through the Grand Canyon. The river is slowed by the Glen Canyon Dam before it flows into the gorge.

Mule deer live in the pine and spruce forests at the top of the canyon. Today there are probably about 10,000 mule deer in the region.

Desert plants, such as this prickly pear cactus, grow low down in the canyon, on dry, flat land above the river.

The diagram below shows the different layers of rock that make up the walls of the canyon. The biggest layer, the Supai Group, is over 1,312 feet thick.

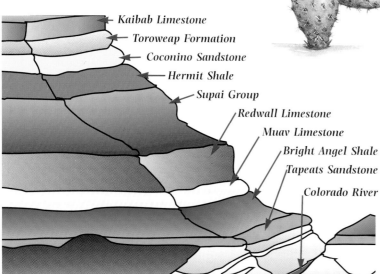

Kaibab Limestone
Toroweap Formation
Coconino Sandstone
Hermit Shale
Supai Group
Redwall Limestone
Muav Limestone
Bright Angel Shale
Tapeats Sandstone
Colorado River

The Kaibab squirrel lives in the pine forest of the canyon's North Rim. It is found nowhere else in the world.

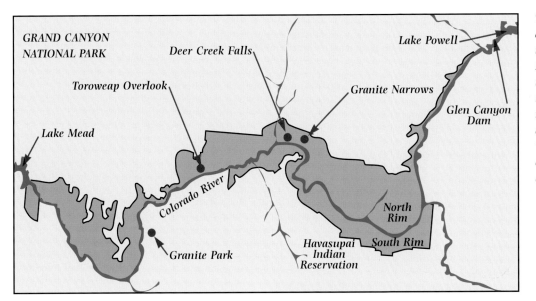

GRAND CANYON
NATIONAL PARK

Deer Creek Falls

Toroweap Overlook

Lake Mead

Colorado River

Granite Park

Lake Powell

Granite Narrows

Glen Canyon
Dam

North
Rim

Havasupai
Indian
Reservation

South Rim

The darker shading
on this map shows
the area of the
National Park around
the Grand Canyon.
Some of the park's
most famous spots
are highlighted.
The lakes at both
ends of the canyon
are formed by dams.

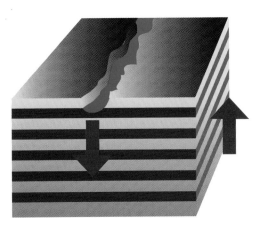

About 4 million years ago, the
Colorado River began to cut a
deep gorge. Movements deep in the
earth have lifted the surrounding
land upward.

Indians of the region made many rock paintings and carvings.
This canyon rock was carved by people of the Ute tribe.

During the last million years,
the top of the Grand Canyon has
continued to move up as the river
carves deeper and deeper.

This view of the South Rim shows the variety of colors and shapes
of the canyon's rock layers.

Great Barrier Reef

This great series of coral reefs lies in the Pacific Ocean, off the coast of Queensland, Australia. The reefs stretch for 1,259 miles along the line of the coast, forming a barrier between the shallow coastal waters and the open sea. Corals belong to the animal family, so the Great Barrier Reef is the largest living structure on earth.

HOW CORAL REEFS GROW

Many corals look like plants, and people used to think this is what they were. But they are really made up of tiny, colorful animals, related to sea anemones and jellyfish. A reef is formed by millions of these creatures, called polyps, which live together in **colonies**. The polyp has a soft body inside a hard, cup-shaped skeleton of limestone. When polyps die, the skeleton remains, and other polyps build on top. This is how coral reefs grow.

LIFE ON THE REEF

Tiny plants called **algae** live inside the coral. They need sunlight to grow and to make food for themselves and the coral. This is why reefs only grow well in shallow water where light can reach. Algae also give coral much of their color.

There are 400 different kinds of coral on the Barrier Reef, with many different shapes, sizes, and colors. Those on the outer edges of the reef are more rubbery and have to withstand the constant pounding of the surf. The more delicate corals are found in calmer waters. The reef provides shelter, food, and oxygen for other forms of life too. There are over 1,400 species of fish, as well as squid and octopus and thousands of different types of shellfish, including giant clams.

MARINE PARK

Coral reefs form some of the rarest and most beautiful natural structures on earth. The largest marine park in the world covers nearly 1,242 miles of the Great Barrier Reef and was created to protect the reef. A system of zones means that some parts are protected from all human activity, while other parts of the reef are used for scientific research or controlled fishing. The reef is popular with divers and snorkelers, and there are organized trips in glass-bottomed boats. Coral reefs are easily damaged by collectors, and it is now illegal to break off coral or take anything away from the reef.

BALANCE OF NATURE

The many forms of animal and plant life around the Great Barrier Reef exist in a delicate balance. This balance can easily be upset. In the 1960's, and again in the 1980's, large sections of the reef were eaten by crown-of-thorns starfish. The numbers of starfish may have grown because people stripped the reef of the shells of sea snails that eat them. There are fewer starfish now, but parts of the Great Barrier Reef may take hundreds of years to recover.

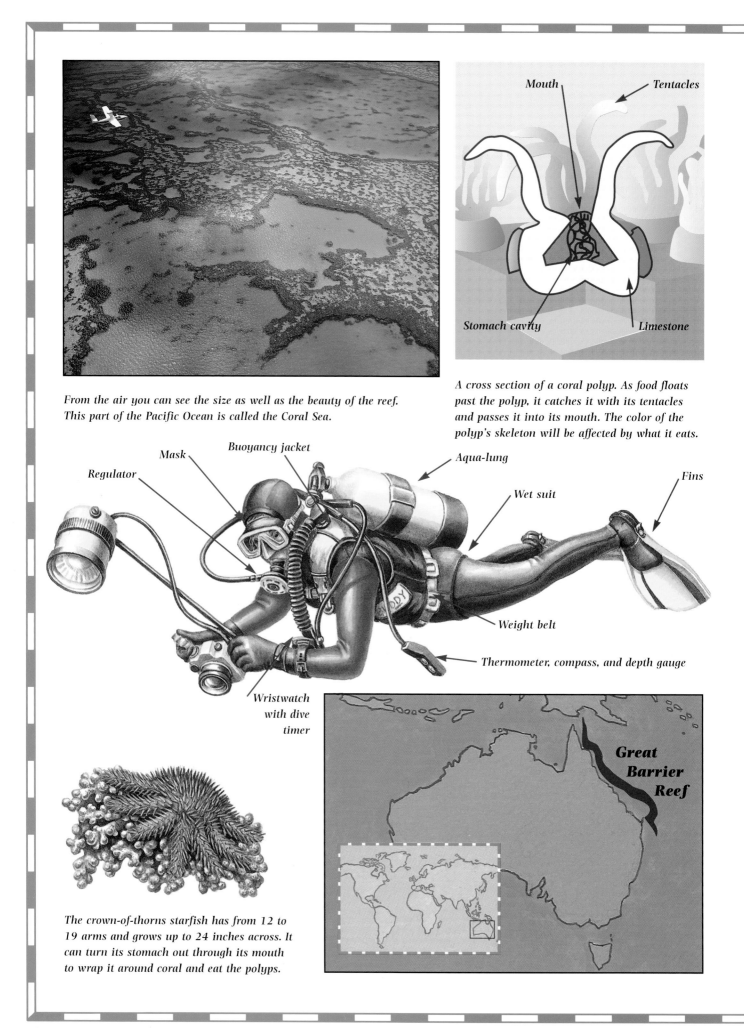

From the air you can see the size as well as the beauty of the reef. This part of the Pacific Ocean is called the Coral Sea.

Mouth

Tentacles

Stomach cavity

Limestone

A cross section of a coral polyp. As food floats past the polyp, it catches it with its tentacles and passes it into its mouth. The color of the polyp's skeleton will be affected by what it eats.

Mask

Buoyancy jacket

Regulator

Aqua-lung

Wet suit

Fins

Weight belt

Thermometer, compass, and depth gauge

Wristwatch with dive timer

Great Barrier Reef

The crown-of-thorns starfish has from 12 to 19 arms and grows up to 24 inches across. It can turn its stomach out through its mouth to wrap it around coral and eat the polyps.

Small coral islands form where the reef is very close to the surface. Heron Island (above) is less than a mile long.

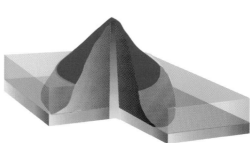

A coral reef sometimes begins around an island formed by the top of an underwater volcano.

As the land sinks over thousands of years, the coral reef goes on growing. Above the water it forms coral islands.

The white-tipped reef shark feeds on smaller fish in the deeper regions. Tiger and whale sharks are also found on the reef.

When the volcano has disappeared, the coral islands are left to form a ring around a **lagoon**. This is called an atoll.

The triton is a sea snail with a spiral shell. It is important to the reef because it feeds on crown-of-thorns starfish.

Parrot fish have teeth that are shaped like curved blades. They use these to scrape coral off the reef and feed on polyps.

Mount Everest

Sir George Everest (1790–1866) was the first to map the mountain that was later named after him.

Everest is the highest mountain in the world. It is one of many high peaks in the Himalayan mountain range, which stretches in a wide curve between northern India and southern China. The Himalayas are the highest mountain range in the world, with more than 100 mountains reaching a height of over 23,951 feet.

THE SUMMIT OF HEAVEN

Mount Everest lies on the border between the small kingdom of Nepal and Tibet. To the people of Tibet, the mountain is known as Qomolongma, which means goddess mother of the world. In Indian it is Sagarmatha, or highest point in heaven. Both names show that this beautiful mountain is also important to the local people.

MOUNTAINS ARE BORN

The Himalayas were formed millions of years ago, when two parts of the earth's outer layer, called its crust, smashed into each other. The earth's crust is made up of pieces, called **plates**, which fit together like a giant jigsaw puzzle. Beneath the hard outer crust, **currents** in the **molten** rock cause these plates to move.

About 45 million years ago, the Indian plate bumped into the larger **Eurasian** plate. The edges of the plates continued to push against each other with enormous force, causing the plates to buckle. This gradually pushed up layers of rock to form mountains. Since that first collision, the Himalayas have been pushed up even farther. Mount Everest gets higher every year, by about 2 inches.

CONQUEST OF EVEREST

The Sherpa people of Nepal live in valleys, high up in the Himalayas. Traditionally they grew crops and herded cattle and yaks. When European mountaineers first tried to climb Everest in the 1920's, they hired Sherpa men to carry their equipment. But they did not make it to the very top, and over the next thirty years several climbers were killed.

In 1953 Edmund Hillary, a beekeeper from New Zealand, and Tenzing Norgay, a Sherpa mountaineer, became the first people to stand on the summit of Mount Everest. Since that historic day, many mountaineers have climbed Everest. In 1992, for example, 32 climbers from five separate expeditions all reached the summit on the same day.

MAPPING MOUNTAINS

People didn't know that Everest was the highest mountain in the world until 1856. Then George Everest, a British **surveyor general**, led an expedition to map the Himalayas. At first the surveyors called the highest mountain in the range, Peak XV. But later it was named after George Everest. Recent surveys have measured the peak at 29,080 feet.

THE ABOMINABLE SNOWMAN

Sherpas tell stories of a large hairy creature reported to live in the mountains. They call it the yeti, or the abominable snowman. It is described as a mysterious manlike creature, over 6 feet tall. Huge footprints have been found, but no one has ever proved that the yeti really exists.

Mountaineers camp in any sheltered spot they can find. This camp is over 22,967 feet up, on the southwest face of Everest.

Oxygen mask

Safety harness

Ice axe

The yak is a large shaggy ox. Some yaks still live wild in the Himalayas at heights up to 19,686 feet.

Many climbers carry oxygen tanks so that they can breathe more easily in the thin air on high mountains.

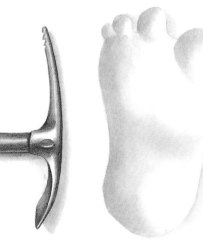

Photographs have been taken of huge footprints on Everest. But most scientists believe the prints are fake.

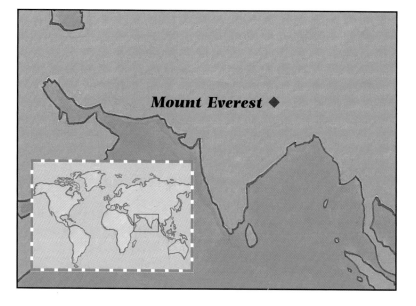

Mount Everest ◆

Shrubs and trees, such as this blooming rhododendron, grow on the lower slopes of the Himalayas.

The snow-capped peaks of the Himalayas, seen in the distance from the lower foothills of Nepal.

Where two plates bump into each other, rocks are folded under pressure and forced upward to make mountains. This is how the Himalayas were formed. They are called fold mountains.

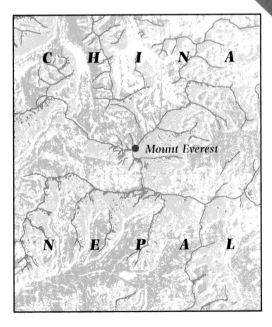

C H I N A

• Mount Everest

N E P A L

Today mapmakers use photographs taken from planes and space **satellites** to chart the Himalayas.

This wild mountain goat, called an ibex, is a sure-footed climber in the high Himalayas.

Sahara Desert

The Sahara is the largest desert in the world, covering more than a quarter of the continent of Africa. It stretches over 3,105 miles from the Atlantic Ocean in the west to the Red Sea in the east. From north to south, the desert extends over 1,397 miles, from the Mediterranean Sea and the Atlas Mountains in the north to Lake Chad in the south. A desert is an area of land where very little or no rain falls. This means that the Sahara is totally dry nearly all the time. The Sahara is also the world's sunniest place, with over 4,300 hours of sunshine a year. Although the desert covers parts of ten different North African countries, fewer than 2 million people live in this barren area.

SHIFTING SANDS

Some parts of the Sahara are entirely made up of shifting sand dunes that have been formed by the strong desert winds. The world's highest dunes are in the Algerian part of the Sahara. They are 1,526 feet high—taller than the Empire State Building in New York.

ROCKY MOUNTAINS

We usually think of deserts as hot, sandy places, but only about a fifth of the Sahara is covered with sand. Some of the desert is made up of flat, stony plains, and much of the rest is covered by rocky uplands. There are also many mountains, such as the Tibesti Mountains in Chad. These mountains are 11,205 feet high, and sometimes there is snow on the peaks.

DESERT WANDERERS

Many of the people of the Sahara are **nomads** wandering the desert from one **oasis** to the next. There are about 90 large oases, where people live in villages and grow crops. But most oases are quite small and can support only one or two families. For centuries the Tuareg people of the central uplands have been nomads, raising herds of sheep, goats, and camels. The men wear robes and a veil across the face. The veil protects them both from desert winds and from the evil spirits that they believe can enter through the mouth. They call themselves Kel Tagilmust, or people of the veil.

An ancient arrowhead (above) found in the Sahara. Thousands of years ago, the region was a rich hunting ground.

SAHARAN WILDLIFE

In the Sahara, in the baking heat of the day, the temperature reaches over 122°F. But at night it can drop dramatically, so that the desert is almost freezing cold. The animals of the Sahara have learned to survive these huge temperature changes. Many animals, such as the desert hedgehog and the fennec fox, live in burrows during the day. They come out to look for food at dusk and dawn, when it is cooler.

THE DROMEDARY

Camels are the largest desert animals and well suited to the hot, dry climate. They are able to survive for weeks without water. They can also store fat in their humps, for reserve energy. Their long eyelashes protect their eyes and they can close their nostrils to keep out the Saharan sand. The Saharan camel is called a dromedary.

Saharan nomads (above) cross the desert with their camels. The Arabian camel is called a dromedary and has only one hump.

Windblown sand has helped to shape these fantastic cliffs and pinnacles in the rocky desert of Algeria.

The desert rose is found on sand dunes. Though it looks like a flower, it is made of a mineral, called gypsum, and sand.

The lanner falcon spots smaller birds, lizards, and insects from a great height as it flies over the desert. Then it swoops down and seizes its prey in its claws. The falcon spends much of the day gliding in the cooler air more than 2,953 feet above the desert.

The fennec of the Sahara is the world's smallest fox. Its enormous ears give off heat, like a radiator. This helps the fox to stay cool.

Scales on the fringe-toed lizard's feet help spread its weight and stop it from sinking into the hot Saharan sand.

This shellfish fossil was found in the Sahara. Millions of years ago, parts of the present-day desert were under the ocean.

This small oasis town lies at the edge of the Sahara's Great Western Erg, a huge area of high, shifting sand dunes.

Crescent-shaped dunes, called barchans, are formed when the desert wind blows the sand mainly from one direction.

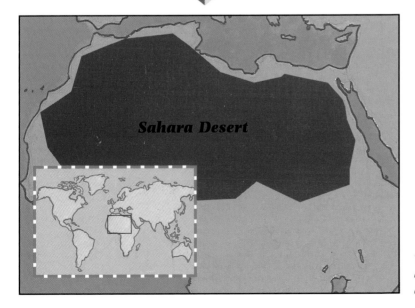

Sahara Desert

Tall date palms often grow in oases. Villagers and nomads eat their sweet fruit, and the leaves and bark are used in making rope and baskets.

Angel Falls

The Angel Falls plunge 3,212 feet from a high **plateau** in the Guiana Highlands of Venezuela, South America. They form the highest waterfall in the world. The total drop is almost twenty times farther than Niagara Falls. The longest single fall is 2,648 feet, which is also the longest in the world. The water falls into a branch of the Carrao River, which then flows into the Caroni River. The Caroni is a **tributary** of the mighty Orinoco River, which it meets as it flows on its way to the Atlantic Ocean.

GUIANA HIGHLANDS

These highlands are full of plateaus, rounded hills, table mountains, and narrow valleys. They stretch across the southeastern region of Venezuela into northern Brazil. The highlands are covered by dense tropical **rain forests** and small areas of **savanna**, or tropical grassland. One of the many separate plateau blocks, or tepuis as they are called locally, is Auyan Tepui. The small cracks and wide **gullies** in the sandstone of the plateau collect an enormous amount of rain. This water spills over the edge of the plateau and creates the Angel Falls.

REDISCOVERY

The falls were "discovered" in the 1930's, although local Indian tribes had known about them for many centuries. In 1935 an American pilot named Jimmy Angel was flying his plane in the region, on the lookout for gold in the hills. When he saw streams cascading down the Auyan Tepui, Angel was sure he was looking at the mightiest waterfall in the world.

RETURN JOURNEY

Angel returned to the falls with his wife and a mountain explorer. He managed to land his plane in a bog at the top of the plateau, but they were unable to reach the top of the falls or take off again. It was two weeks before they turned up at their base camp on foot.

SCIENTIFIC SURVEY

Fourteen years later the Angel Falls, now named after the intrepid pilot, were properly surveyed. An expedition traveled up the river to the falls in motorized canoes. Jimmy Angel was proved right: the waterfall was the highest in the world. Jimmy was killed in an air crash in 1956, and his ashes were scattered over the Angel Falls. His original plane can now be seen in a Venezuelan museum.

THE FALLS TODAY

The area around the falls is still covered with dense jungle and savanna, although there is a tourist lodge and hotel at nearby Canaima. From there the only way to see the Angel Falls is to go on a boat or plane trip.

EL DORADO

Some people believe that the mythical city of El Dorado lay in the Guiana Highlands. According to legend, the city was paved with gold. El Dorado, which means "golden man," was the ruler of the city. He was so rich that he covered his body with gold dust every morning. Many explorers have searched for the city but without success. Historians now believe that El Dorado probably never existed.

This sundew plant (above) grows on Auyan Tepui. Its sticky leaves trap insects, which the plant digests.

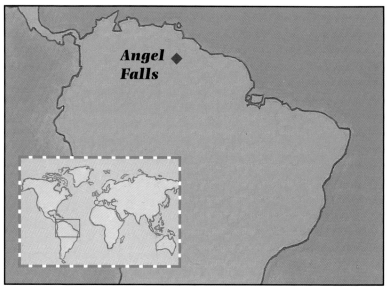

Angel
Falls

Jimmy Angel was looking for gold.
Small gold nuggets like this one
(right) can be washed out of
the rock and downstream
by fast-flowing rivers.

During the rainy
season, the Angel Falls
are at their fullest and
the water thunders
down. Then the
summit is often
hidden by clouds
and water spray.

The giant otter lives in the region's rivers,
feeding on fish, eggs, and birds. From nose
to tail it grows to over 6 feet long.

The pygmy marsupial frog lives among the
tepui plants. The female keeps her eggs in
a skin pouch on her back.

Some of the world's toughest plants grow right on top of the tepuis.
Most are found only in this region.

The tepuis of the Guiana Highlands (left) are covered in plant life. They are what remain of a vast sandstone plateau that has been eroded over millions of years. The lower slopes are covered in rain forest.

Jimmy Angel's plane, El Rio Caroni (below). It was taken from the top of Auyan Tepui 34 years after he landed it there.

A typical tepui of the region (below) might rise over 4,922 feet above the surrounding forest. Tepui is a local Indian word for mountain.

Sarawak Chamber

The world's largest cave **chamber** was discovered in 1980 on the island of Borneo in Southeast Asia. The vast Sarawak Chamber is part of a huge network of limestone caves at the foot of Gunung (or Mount) Api. The chamber is big enough to hold twenty-three football pitches.

CAVE EXPLORATION

In 1980 a group of explorers were inside a long underground passage when they suddenly came upon a vast cavern. The cave was too big to be lit by their lamps, and it took them twelve hours to explore its entire length.

MAPPING THE CAVES

The cavers quickly realized that they had found the largest underground cavern in the world. The Sarawak Chamber is 2,297 feet long and an average of 984 feet wide. The ceiling ranges in height from 230 to 394 feet.

Since the Sarawak Chamber was discovered, explorers have mapped many more of the caves in the network, which wind more than 124 miles beneath the mountain. An underground passage, 47 miles long, links Clearwater Cave, which has a low river running through it, to the Cave of the Winds. Many of the caves are now open to the public.

HOW THE CAVES WERE FORMED

Borneo lies on the equator, so it is always warm. There is rain all year around, and it is very wet during the **monsoon** season, from October to March. Over millions of years, rainwater has poured along the huge ridge beneath the slopes of Gunung Api. This ridge is made of limestone, which is a soft rock. Because rainwater contains a weak acid, it has dissolved the limestone and formed caves under the mountain.

NATIONAL PARK

The state of Sarawak, in the northwest of Borneo, belongs to Malaysia. Today the whole area, including the caves, has been made into a national park. Many animals live in the park, including one of the smallest mammals in the world—the pygmy shrew.

THE MOUNTAINS

The limestone mountain of Gunung Api rises to a height of 5,742 feet. It lies very close to Sarawak's second highest peak, Gunung Mulu, which gives the National Park its name. Gunung Mulu, which is 7,799 feet high, is part of a range of sandstone and shale mountains. Both Api and Mulu are over 5 million years old.

LIFE IN THE DARK

Although it is dark, damp,j and cold inside the caves beneath Gunung Api, some creatures spend their whole lives here. Many of them are almost colorless. There are poisonous scorpions, semitransparent crabs, blind spiders, and white snakes. Colonies of bats hang from the cave roofs during the day and leave at night to hunt for food. Swiftlets also build their nests in the caves.

This old cave entrance, over 328 feet high, once led to Sarawak Chamber. Rock falls have since blocked its passage.

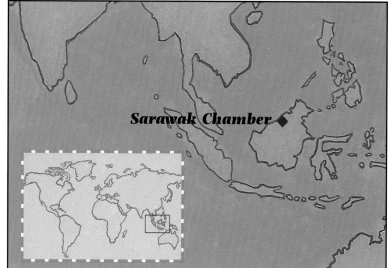

Sarawak Chamber ◆

Cavers wear protective, waterproof clothing. Sometimes the caves, and the tunnels that link them, are flooded, and there is danger from falling rocks.

Protective headgear

Flashlight

Battery pack

Safety harness

Waterproof boots

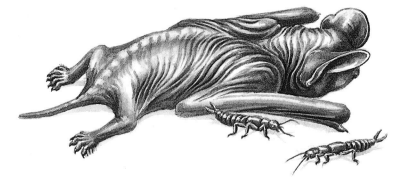

Naked bats live in the Sarawak caves. Hairy earwigs help to keep them clean by eating tiny parasites that live on them.

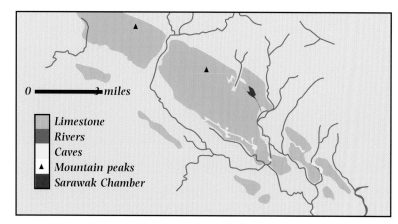

0 ▬▬▬ 3 miles

■ Limestone
■ Rivers
□ Caves
▲ Mountain peaks
■ Sarawak Chamber

The map shows the location of Sarawak Chamber. Gunung Mulu National Park covers a total area of 210 square miles.

(Above) Sarawak Chamber. The scenery is dramatic. The limestone pinnacles near the summit of Gunung Api are razor-edged, and up to 164 feet high.

Huntsman spiders live in the Sarawak caves. They have very long legs and a total leg span of 6 inches.

This crosssection through limestone rocks shows how water runs down to form caves. A cave system like this may take thousands of years to form.

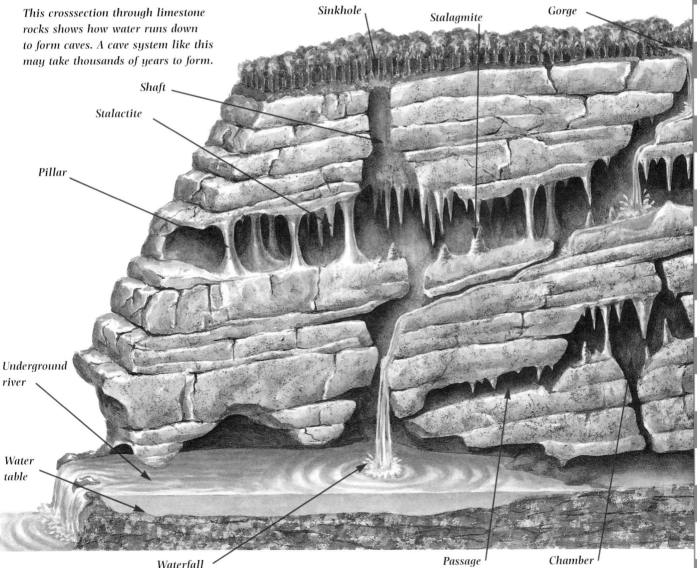

Sinkhole

Stalagmite

Gorge

Shaft

Stalactite

Pillar

Underground river

Water table

Waterfall

Passage

Chamber

Mauna Loa

Mauna Loa, which means "long mountain," is the largest **active** volcano in the world. Its wide slopes cover a large part of the island of Hawaii, and it rises to 13,682 feet above sea level. The volcano's **crater**, called Mokuaweoweo, covers over 4 square miles and is 591 feet deep. This huge volcano could erupt at any time. The last major eruption was in 1984, and Mauna Loa rumbled loudly in 1988.

VOLCANIC ISLANDS

Mauna Loa is one of two active volcanoes on Hawaii, which is the largest of a chain of islands in the North Pacific Ocean. The rest of the Hawaiian islands are the tips of old, **extinct** volcanoes.

A NEW ISLAND

All the Hawaiian island volcanoes were formed in the same way. The ocean floor moves slowly over a very hot area in the earth's **mantle**, which contains molten rock. The hot spot erupts **lava** onto the seabed. Over thousands of years, layers of lava build up to form an underwater mountain with gently sloping sides. This type of volcano is known as a shield volcano, because it is shaped like an upturned shield. Mauna Loa is this shape and was made in this way. Mauna Loa continued to grow until it emerged from the sea, probably around 500,000 years ago.

Pele (above) is the Hawaiian goddess of volcanoes. Legend says she lives in a volcanic crater near Mauna Loa.

A GROWING VOLCANO

Mauna Loa is over 29,529 feet high when measured from the ocean bed. This is higher than Mount Everest. But scientists think that the volcano may be nearing the end of its growing life. Each year it moves about 39 inches away from the hot spot.

There is a younger active volcano, Kilauea, nearby. A third, Loihi, is growing under the sea to the south. It is usually safe to watch the constant, but less powerful eruptions of Kilauea.

ERUPTION

Mauna Loa erupts, on average, once every four years. In 1935 a big eruption caused a huge river of lava to flow toward the island's main city, Hilo, over 31 miles away. U.S. Army planes dropped bombs in the path of the lava flow to save the town.

In 1950 a 12-mile-long crack threw out even more lava, which flowed from the volcano for 23 days and destroyed a small village. Another eruption, in 1984, again threatened the people of Hilo. This time the lava flow covered 9 miles in its first day. The molten river changed course just before it reached the city.

LIVING WITH VOLCANOES

Mauna Loa is a magnificent example of the earth's natural power. We cannot stop volcanoes erupting, but we can learn more about them and be prepared for emergencies. On Hawaii, barriers have been built to divert lava flows around the villages. There is also a scientific base where scientists try to work out, in advance, when eruptions may occur.

Mauna Loa has vast sloping sides that reach from its peak to the Pacific Coast, 20 miles away.

This long lava stalagmite was made by molten lava dripping from the roof of a volcanic cave.

Molten lava is sometimes blown into fine threads. When they turn solid (above), they are called Pele's hair, after the Hawaiian goddess.

Scientists who study volcanoes are called volcanologists. They wear heat-reflecting, protective suits. The long rod is used to collect lava, which will give them information about the volcano.

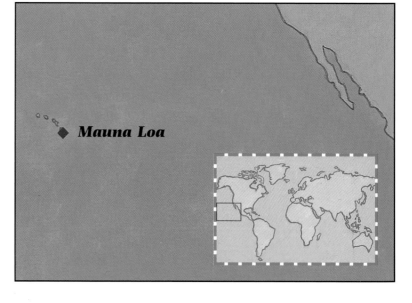

Mauna Loa

Smooth, ropy lava is known by its Hawaiian name, pahoehoe (pronounced pa-hoy-hoy).

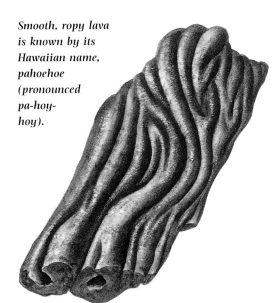

Mauna Loa erupts. On Hawaiian volcanoes, molten lava often spurts from long cracks to make a curtain of fire.

How a hot spot creates volcanic islands (right), as the ocean floor moves over it. Each volcano stays over the hot spot for about a million years.

When lava cools very quickly, it may form pumice (above). Pumice is full of air holes, created by gases escaping from the lava as it cools. It is so light that it floats on water. People use its rough surface to clean their skin.

Sometimes pahoehoe flows form a red-hot tunnel beneath the cooling surface. These volcanic caves are known as lava tubes.

GLOSSARY

active: (of a volcano) that may erupt at any time.

algae: tiny plants like seaweed.

chamber: a large room in a cave system.

colony: a group of animals that live together.

crater: a bowl-shaped opening at the top of a volcano.

crust: the earth's outer shell.

current: a strong, steady flow in one direction.

dune: a high mound of sand.

Eurasian: combining the continents of Europe and Asia.

extinct: (of a volcano) no longer active; dead.

gully: a channel cut by moving water.

heritage: evidence of the past inherited by people today.

lagoon: a body of water cut off from the open sea.

lava: molten rock thrown out of a volcano.

mantle: the layer of rock that lies beneath the earth's crust.

molten: melted; turned into liquid.

monsoon: heavy rains brought by a seasonal wind (also called monsoon).

national park: an area that people visit where animals, plants, and land are protected.

nomads: people who wander from place to place to find food and grazing land for their animals.

oasis: an area in a desert with water, where plants can grow and people live.

plate: a huge piece of the earth's crust.

plateau: a flat area of high land.

rain forest: thick forest found in warm tropical areas of heavy rainfall.

reservation: an area of land set aside for Native American people.

satellite: a device that circles the earth in space and sends back information.

savanna: grassland with scattered bushes or trees.

scrub: scattered plants in a dry region.

shale: a dark rock formed from clay.

surveyor general: the official leader of a team measuring and mapping land.

tributary: a small river that flows into a larger one.

INDEX

First published in hardback edition in 2001 by Chelsea House Publishers, a subsidiary of Haights Cross Communications. All rights reserved. Printed and bound in China.

First published in the UK in 1996 by Belitha Press Limited, London House, Great Eastern Wharf, Parkgate Road, London SW11 4NQ, England

Text copyright © Belitha Press Limited 1996
Series devised and designed by Reg Cox
Text by Neil Morris
Illustrators copyright © James Field 1996
Editor: Claire Edwards
Picture Researcher: Diana Morris
Consultant: Steve Pollock

First printing
1 3 5 7 9 8 6 4 2

The Chelsea House World Wide Web address is http://www.chelseahouse.com

Library of Congress Cataloging-in-Publication Data applied for.

ISBN: 0-7910-6049-7

Picture acknowledgments:
Mountain Camera: 14 top John Cleare. South American Pictures: 23 top Tony Morrison. Still Pictures: 18 top Bios/George Lopez, 19 top Frans Lemmens. Tony Waltham: 26 top, 27 top. Zefa: front cover Sojo, 6 top left Allstock, 7 bottom, 10 top Foley, 11 top Bell, 15 top, 22 top Sojo, 30 top, 31 top, 31 top Pacific Stock.